TALES THAT SELL:

How to Use Storytelling to Build Your Brand and Grow Your Business

Daniel C. Partin

Table of content

Introduction

Welcome to the exciting world of storytelling for business growth! In today's fast-paced and ever-changing business landscape, it is no longer enough to simply sell a product or service. To succeed in this competitive environment, businesses must connect with their customers on a deeper level and establish a strong emotional connection. This is where the power of storytelling comes in.

Storytelling has been a fundamental part of human communication for centuries. From ancient cave paintings to modern-day Hollywood blockbusters, stories have always been a powerful way to engage, educate, and entertain. When used in the context of business, storytelling can be a game-changer. It allows businesses to create a compelling brand narrative, establish an emotional connection with their customers, and differentiate themselves from their competitors.

In this book, we will explore the art and science of storytelling for business growth. We will delve into the psychology behind storytelling and how it can be used to influence consumer behavior. We will examine the various types of stories that businesses can use to engage their audience and build their brand. We will also explore the different mediums through which stories can be told, such as social media, video marketing, and public speaking.

But storytelling is not just about entertaining your audience or creating a compelling brand narrative. It is also a powerful tool for sales. Through effective storytelling, businesses can overcome objections, build trust with their customers, and ultimately drive sales. We will explore the different techniques and strategies that businesses can use to leverage the power of storytelling to boost their sales and grow their business.

Whether you are a small business owner or a marketing professional, this book is for you. By the end of this book, you will have a deep understanding of the power of storytelling, how it can be used to boost sales and grow your business, and the tools and techniques you need to create compelling stories that resonate with your audience. So, let's dive into the world of storytelling for business growth and unlock the full potential of your business!

The Power of Storytelling in Sales

Storytelling is a powerful tool in sales that can help connect with potential customers on an emotional level and drive them to make a purchase. When done correctly, storytelling can help differentiate a product or service from competitors, establish trust and credibility, and create a memorable experience for the customer.

Here are some ways in which the power of storytelling can be leveraged in sales:

Establishing a connection with the customer: A good story can help establish a connection with the customer by creating a relatable experience or emotion. By sharing a personal story, the salesperson can make the customer feel understood and build a sense of trust and empathy.

Differentiating from competitors: In a crowded market, storytelling can help differentiate a product or service by highlighting unique features and benefits. By telling a story that showcases the product or service's strengths, the salesperson can convince the customer to choose their offering over a competitor's.

Creating a memorable experience: People are more likely to remember a story than a list of features and benefits. By telling a story that resonates with the customer, the salesperson can create a memorable experience that the customer will associate with the product or service.

Overcoming objections: Storytelling can also be used to overcome objections or concerns that the customer may have. By telling a story about how the product or service has helped other customers overcome similar challenges, the salesperson can address the customer's concerns and build confidence in the offering.

Fostering loyalty: Storytelling can also be used to foster long-term loyalty with customers. By regularly sharing stories about the product or service and how it's making a positive impact, the salesperson can build a relationship with the customer that goes beyond a one-time transaction.

When using storytelling in sales, it's important to keep in mind the following tips:

Know your audience: Tailor your stories to your audience and their specific needs and interests.

Keep it concise: Keep your stories short and to the point. You don't want to lose your customer's attention.

Make it relatable: Use stories that your customers can relate to and that evoke an emotional response.

Be authentic: Don't make up stories or exaggerate the truth. Customers can sense when someone is being disingenuous.

Practice: Practice your storytelling skills and get feedback from others to improve.

The power of storytelling in sales cannot be underestimated. By using stories to establish a connection, differentiate from competitors, create a memorable experience, overcome objections, and foster loyalty, salespeople can create a more effective and engaging sales experience for their customers.

The Purpose and Benefits of Storyselling

Storyselling is the art of using storytelling to sell a product, service, or idea. It involves weaving a narrative around the product, highlighting its features and benefits in a way that captures the attention and imagination of the customer. Storyselling is a powerful tool for marketers and salespeople, as it helps to create an emotional connection with the customer and makes them more likely to buy.

The purpose of storyselling is to create a compelling story that resonates with the customer and motivates them to take action. Storyselling is not about tricking or manipulating the customer, but rather about creating a genuine connection and building trust. By telling a story that highlights the benefits of the product or service, the customer is more likely to see the value in what is being offered and make a purchase.

There are several benefits of storyselling that make it an effective sales technique:

Captures Attention: People are naturally drawn to stories. By telling a story that is relevant and interesting, you capture the customer's attention and make them more receptive to what you have to say.

Engages Emotions: Stories are a powerful tool for engaging emotions. By creating an emotional connection with the customer, you increase the likelihood that they will remember your message and take action.

Simplifies Complex Ideas: Storytelling is an effective way to simplify complex ideas and make them more accessible to the customer. By breaking down complicated concepts into a narrative, you make it easier for the customer to understand the benefits of the product or service.

Builds Trust: By telling a story that is honest and transparent, you build trust with the customer. This trust is essential for establishing a long-term relationship and creating repeat business.

Increases Sales: Ultimately, the goal of storyselling is to increase sales. By creating a compelling story that resonates with the customer, you increase the likelihood that they will make a purchase.

To be effective at storyselling, it is important to understand the needs and motivations of the customer. The story should be tailored to the customer's interests and values, and should highlight the specific benefits of the product or service that are most important to them. It is also important to be authentic and honest in the storytelling process, as customers are more likely to trust and connect with a genuine story..

Another important aspect of storyselling is the use of visuals and other sensory elements to bring the story to life. This could include using photos, videos, or other multimedia to create a more immersive experience for the customer. By engaging multiple senses, you can create a more memorable and impactful story.

It's also important to note that the best stories are those that are authentic and genuine. Customers are savvy and can easily spot a fake or inauthentic story. To be effective at storyselling, it's important to be honest and transparent, and to share stories that are rooted in reality.

It's worth noting that storyselling can be used in a variety of contexts beyond just sales. Storytelling can be used to build a brand, to create a culture within an organization, or to inspire people to take action for a cause. By harnessing the power of storytelling, individuals and organizations can create a more compelling message and connect with their audience on a deeper level.

Storyselling is a powerful sales technique that can help businesses to connect with customers, build trust, and increase sales. By creating a compelling narrative that highlights the benefits of the product or service, businesses can engage emotions, simplify complex ideas, and build lasting relationships with customers.

Chapter 1: What is Storyselling?

The Definition of Storyselling

Storyselling is a marketing technique that involves using storytelling to sell a product or service to customers. This approach is based on the idea that people are more likely to remember and connect with a brand when it is presented to them in the form of a story that resonates with them emotionally. Storyselling is a powerful tool that can be used to create a deep emotional connection between a brand and its audience, and to build brand loyalty and trust over time.

At its core, storyselling involves telling a compelling narrative that showcases the unique features and benefits of a product or service, while also addressing the needs and desires of the target audience. The story should be engaging, memorable, and persuasive, and should focus on the key selling points of the product or service in a way that is easy for customers to understand and relate to.

To be effective, a storyselling approach should be based on a deep understanding of the target audience and their motivations. This requires research and analysis to identify the key pain points, desires, and values of the target demographic, and to craft a story that speaks directly to these concerns.

There are many different elements that can be incorporated into a storyselling approach, including:

A strong protagonist: A compelling protagonist can help to anchor the story and make it more relatable and engaging for the audience. This could be a fictional character, or a real-life customer who has benefited from the product or service.

A clear conflict: Every good story needs a conflict or problem to be resolved. In the case of storyselling, the conflict might be a customer's pain point or a challenge that the product or service is uniquely positioned to address.

Emotional resonance: Storyselling is all about creating an emotional connection with the audience. This requires tapping into the core values and desires of the target demographic and framing the product or service in a way that speaks directly to these concerns.

A clear call-to-action: The story should end with a clear call-to-action that encourages customers to take the next step, whether that's making a purchase, signing up for a trial, or contacting the company for more information.

Overall, storyselling is a powerful marketing technique that can be used to build brand awareness, generate leads, and drive sales. By telling a compelling story that resonates with the target audience, companies can create a deep emotional connection with their customers and build long-lasting relationships based on trust and loyalty.

How Storyselling is Different from Traditional Sales

Storyselling, as the name suggests, involves using storytelling to sell a product or service. It is a more effective approach to selling than traditional sales methods because it focuses on the customer's emotions and engages them on a deeper level. Here are some ways in which storyselling differs from traditional sales:

Emotional Appeal: Storyselling focuses on connecting with customers on an emotional level. By telling a story, the salesperson can create an emotional connection with the customer and help them visualize how the product or service can benefit them. In contrast, traditional sales methods focus on logic and features, which may not resonate with the customer on an emotional level.

Building Trust: Storyselling is an effective way of building trust with the customer. By sharing a story, the salesperson can demonstrate their understanding of the customer's needs and build rapport with them. Traditional sales methods, on the other hand, can come across as pushy and insincere, which can erode trust.

Engaging the Customer: Storyselling is a more engaging approach to selling. By telling a story, the salesperson can capture the customer's attention and keep them engaged throughout the sales process. In contrast, traditional sales methods can be monotonous and fail to hold the customer's attention.

Creating a Memorable Experience: Storyselling creates a memorable experience for the customer. By telling a compelling story, the salesperson can leave a lasting impression on the customer, which can increase the likelihood of a sale. In contrast, traditional sales methods can be forgettable and fail to make an impact.

Personalization: Storyselling can be personalized to the customer's needs. By tailoring the story to the customer's specific situation, the salesperson can create a more relevant and personalized experience for the customer. Traditional sales methods can be generic and fail to address the customer's specific needs.

Storyselling is a more effective approach to selling than traditional sales methods because it focuses on the customer's emotions, builds trust, engages the customer, creates a memorable experience, and can be personalized to the customer's needs. By incorporating storytelling into the sales process, salespeople can connect with customers on a deeper level and increase the likelihood of a sale.

Why Storyselling Works

Storyselling is the process of using stories to sell products, services, or ideas. It is a powerful marketing strategy that has gained traction in recent years, especially with the rise of social media and content marketing. Storyselling works because it leverages the power of storytelling to create an emotional connection with the audience, building trust, and ultimately driving sales.

To understand why storyselling works, it is important to first understand the power of storytelling. Stories have been used for centuries to communicate ideas, values, and beliefs. From ancient myths to modern-day advertising, stories have the ability to captivate and engage audiences, transporting them to different worlds and evoking strong emotions.

One reason why stories are so powerful is that they activate multiple areas of the brain. Research has shown that when we hear a story, our brains light up in a way that is different from when we hear a list of facts or statistics. This is because stories engage both the left and right hemispheres of the brain, activating sensory, motor, and emotional regions. This leads to a deeper and more memorable experience for the listener.

Another reason why stories are effective is that they allow us to see things from a different perspective. Stories have the ability to transport us to different worlds, times, and places, allowing us to experience things that we might not be able to in our everyday lives. This helps us to broaden our understanding of the world and empathize with others.

Now, let's dive into why storyselling works specifically:

Stories create an emotional connection

One of the key reasons why storyselling is effective is that it creates an emotional connection with the audience. When we hear a story, we are able to relate to the characters and their experiences. This helps us to feel more connected to the brand or product being sold.

For example, imagine a company that sells outdoor gear. Instead of just listing the features of their products, they tell the story of a family who went on a camping trip and how their gear helped them to have a great time. This story helps the audience to see themselves in the shoes of the family and imagine how the product could enhance their own outdoor experiences.

Stories build trust

Another reason why storyselling works is that it helps to build trust with the audience. When a brand tells a story, they are showing that they understand their audience's needs and desires. This helps to establish a sense of credibility and authenticity, which is important in building trust.

For example, a company that sells organic skincare products could tell the story of how their founder struggled with skin issues and was unable to find products that worked for them. They could then explain how they decided to create their own products and how they have helped others with similar issues. By sharing this story, the brand is showing that they are not just trying to sell a product, but that they have a deeper understanding of their audience's needs and have created a solution based on personal experience.

Stories are memorable

Another reason why storyselling is effective is that stories are more memorable than other types of content. When we hear a story, we are more likely to remember it because it engages multiple areas of the brain and creates an emotional connection.

For example, imagine a company that sells energy drinks. Instead of just listing the benefits of their product, they tell the story of a professional athlete who uses their drink to power through their workouts. This story is more memorable than a list of benefits because it creates a visual and emotional experience for the audience.

Stories create a call to action

Storyselling is effective because it creates a call to action. When a brand tells a story, they are not just trying to entertain their audience; they are trying to persuade them to take action. This could be to buy a product, sign up for a service, or share the story with others. A good story will create a sense of urgency and make the audience feel like they need to take action.

For example, a company that sells fitness equipment could tell the story of a customer who was able to transform their body and improve their health with the help of their products. The story could include the challenges the customer faced, such as lack of motivation or a busy schedule, and how the products helped them to overcome those challenges. By sharing this story, the brand is creating a call to action for the audience to take control of their health and fitness by buying the products.

Storyselling works because it leverages the power of storytelling to create an emotional connection with the audience, build trust, create a memorable experience, and ultimately persuade the audience to take action. By using stories to sell products, services, or ideas, brands can differentiate themselves from the competition and create a deeper and more meaningful relationship with their audience.

Chapter 2: The Science of Storytelling

The Psychology of Storytelling

The psychology of storytelling is a fascinating area of study that explores how stories impact human emotions, thoughts, and behavior. Stories have been a fundamental part of human culture for thousands of years and have been used to convey knowledge, entertain, and inspire. As such, understanding the psychological underpinnings of storytelling can help us appreciate the power of narratives and how they shape our experiences.

One of the primary reasons why stories are so powerful is that they tap into our innate human need for connection and meaning. We are social creatures, and stories allow us to relate to others and feel a sense of belonging. This is because stories often feature characters that we can empathize with, and their struggles and triumphs can resonate with our own experiences.

Moreover, stories are effective at influencing our emotions and attitudes. Research has shown that when we engage with stories, our brains release oxytocin, a hormone associated with bonding and empathy. This means that stories can help us develop greater empathy and understanding of others. Additionally, stories can also influence our attitudes and beliefs, as they can challenge our preconceptions and encourage us to see things from a different perspective.

Another reason why stories are so powerful is that they can transport us to different worlds and realities. When we read a book or watch a movie, we become immersed in the story and can lose ourselves in the narrative. This can be an incredibly powerful experience, as it allows us to temporarily escape our own realities and explore new ideas and possibilities.

In addition to the emotional and cognitive effects of storytelling, there are also physical benefits. Studies have shown that when we engage with stories, our bodies can respond as if we are experiencing the events ourselves. This means that stories can activate the same neural pathways and physiological responses as real-life experiences, which can have therapeutic benefits. For example, storytelling has been used in therapeutic settings to help people overcome trauma and promote healing.

Overall, the psychology of storytelling is a complex and multifaceted area of study that highlights the power of narratives to influence our emotions, attitudes, and behaviors. By understanding the psychological mechanisms that underlie storytelling, we can appreciate the importance of stories in human culture and explore their potential to inspire, educate, and heal.

How Stories Affect the Brain

Stories have been an integral part of human communication since ancient times. From the earliest cave paintings to modern-day films, stories have been used to convey ideas, teach lessons, and entertain people. But, have you ever wondered how stories affect the brain? Let's explore this question in detail.

The Brain and Stories

The brain is a complex organ that is responsible for a wide range of functions, including perception, movement, emotion, and cognition. When we hear or read a story, different areas of the brain are activated. Studies have shown that a story activates not only the language centers of the brain but also many other areas, including the sensory and motor areas, the emotional centers, and the areas responsible for social cognition and empathy.

The Power of Narratives
Narratives have a unique power to capture our attention and engage us emotionally. When we hear a story, our brains start to create a mental image of the story's events and characters. This mental simulation is often so vivid that it can be difficult to distinguish between what is real and what is imaginary. This immersion in the story is what makes it so compelling and memorable.

Emotional Engagement
Emotions play a crucial role in the way stories affect our brains. When we are

emotionally engaged with a story, our brains release a chemical called oxytocin. Oxytocin is sometimes referred to as the "love hormone" because it is associated with feelings of trust, empathy, and connection. This chemical reinforces the emotional connection between the listener or reader and the story, making it more memorable and impactful.

Empathy and Social Cognition

Stories also play a role in developing empathy and social cognition. When we hear a story, we are often transported into the shoes of the protagonist, experiencing their joys and struggles. This experience of perspective-taking helps us to develop our empathy skills, allowing us to better understand and connect with others. Additionally, stories often contain social cues and references that help us to navigate social situations more effectively.

Memory Consolidation

Finally, stories have been shown to play a role in memory consolidation. When we hear a story, our brains are more likely to remember the information that is presented within the context of the story. This is because the story provides a framework for organizing and storing the information in a more meaningful way. This is why we often remember the plot and characters of a book or movie long after we have forgotten specific details.

Stories have a powerful effect on the brain. They engage us emotionally, develop our empathy and social cognition skills, and help us to consolidate and remember information. The next time you hear a story, pay attention to the way your brain responds. You may be surprised at how deeply stories affect us.

The Components of a Good Story

A good story is a well-constructed narrative that captures the reader's attention and takes them on a journey through a series of events. It can be fictional or non-fictional, but regardless of its genre, there are certain elements that are essential for a good story. Here are some of the key components of a good story:

Characters: Characters are the driving force of any story. They can be real or fictional, but they must be well-developed, relatable, and interesting. Readers should care about what happens to them and be invested in their journey.

Plot: The plot is the sequence of events that makes up the story. It should be well-structured, with a clear beginning, middle, and end. The plot should also have a clear conflict or problem that the characters must overcome.

Setting: The setting is the time and place in which the story takes place. It should be well-described and provide context for the events of the story. The setting can also play a role in the plot, creating obstacles or opportunities for the characters.

Theme: The theme is the underlying message or idea of the story. It can be implicit or explicit, but it should be meaningful and resonate with readers. A good theme can help readers connect with the story on a deeper level.

Dialogue: Dialogue is the spoken or written words of the characters. It should be natural and believable, revealing information about the characters and advancing the plot. Good dialogue can also add depth and complexity to the characters.

Point of view: The point of view is the perspective from which the story is told. It can be first-person, third-person, or omniscient. The point of view should be consistent throughout the story and should be chosen carefully to enhance the reader's understanding of the characters and events.

Conflict: Conflict is the tension or struggle that drives the plot forward. It can be external, such as a physical obstacle or antagonist, or internal, such as a character's inner turmoil. A good story should have a clear and compelling conflict that keeps the reader engaged.

Resolution: The resolution is the end of the story, where the conflict is resolved and loose ends are tied up. It should be satisfying and provide closure for the reader.

Overall, a good story should be well-crafted, engaging, and memorable. By incorporating these key components, writers can create a story that resonates with readers and leaves a lasting impact.

Chapter 3: Identifying Your Target Audience

Understanding Your Ideal Customer

Understanding your ideal customer is essential for any business that wants to succeed. Without a clear understanding of who your target audience is, it can be challenging to create effective marketing campaigns, develop products or services that resonate with them, and ultimately, drive sales.

Here are some key considerations to help you understand your ideal customer:

Demographics: Start by understanding the basic demographic information about your ideal customer. This includes age, gender, location, income level, education level, marital status, and occupation. This information can help you develop a broad picture of your target audience.

Psychographics: Understanding the psychographics of your ideal customer is equally important. This includes their values, beliefs, attitudes, interests, and lifestyle choices. Psychographic information can help you create marketing messages that resonate with your audience on a deeper level.

Pain Points: Identify the problems and challenges that your ideal customer faces. This information can help you develop products and services that solve their problems, and create marketing campaigns that speak directly to their pain points.

Buying Behavior: Understand how your ideal customer makes purchasing decisions. This includes their purchasing habits, motivations, and decision-making criteria. This information can help you create effective marketing campaigns and sales strategies.

Communication Channels: Identify the channels that your ideal customer uses to communicate and consume information. This includes social media platforms, email, search engines, and other digital channels. Knowing where your audience is active can help you create targeted marketing campaigns that reach them where they are.

Competitive Landscape: Understand your competition and how they are targeting the same audience. Analyze their marketing strategies, product offerings, and customer experience to identify opportunities for differentiation.

By understanding your ideal customer, you can create marketing campaigns and products that resonate with them on a deep level, which can ultimately lead to increased sales and business growth. Don't be afraid to ask your customers for feedback and use data to inform your decisions. By constantly refining your understanding of your ideal customer, you can stay ahead of the competition and build a loyal customer base.

Developing Buyer Personas

Developing buyer personas is an essential step in creating a successful marketing strategy for any business. A buyer persona is a semi-fictional representation of your ideal customer based on market research and real data about your existing customers. This persona provides insights into the motivations, goals, and behaviors of your target audience, enabling you to tailor your marketing efforts to better resonate with them. In this response, we will discuss comprehensively the steps to developing buyer personas.

Conduct Market Research: Before creating buyer personas, it's crucial to gather information about your target audience. You can conduct surveys, interviews, and focus groups to collect data on their demographics, behavior patterns, pain points, and goals.

Identify Common Characteristics: Analyze the data collected from your market research to identify commonalities among your customers. Look for shared demographics, such as age, gender, and income, as well as shared interests, values, and behaviors.

Create Persona Profiles: Once you have identified the commonalities among your customers, it's time to create persona profiles. Each profile should be a detailed description of your ideal customer, including their demographics, behavior patterns, pain points, and goals. Give your persona a name, job title, and image to make it more relatable.

Use the Right Tools: To create accurate buyer personas, you can use tools such as surveys, interviews, and analytics software. There are also online tools such as HubSpot and MakeMyPersona that provide templates for creating buyer personas.

Refine and Test: Refine your buyer personas by incorporating feedback from your customers, sales team, and other stakeholders. Test your personas by using them to develop marketing campaigns, customer journey maps, and product development strategies.

Use Personas to Guide Marketing Efforts: Once your buyer personas are complete, use them to guide your marketing efforts. Tailor your messaging, advertising, and content to resonate with your target audience. Use your buyer personas to develop marketing campaigns that address their pain points and goals.

Developing buyer personas is an essential step in creating a successful marketing strategy. By gathering data on your target audience and creating persona profiles, you can tailor your marketing efforts to better resonate with your ideal customer. Refine and test your personas and use them to guide your marketing efforts to improve your sales and build customer loyalty.

Researching Your Audience

Researching your audience is a critical component of any successful communication strategy, whether you're delivering a presentation, writing an article, or creating a marketing campaign. Understanding your audience helps you tailor your message to their needs, interests, and expectations, which ultimately leads to better engagement and higher levels of satisfaction.

Here are some key steps to researching your audience:

Identify your audience

The first step in researching your audience is to identify who they are. Ask yourself: Who are the people you're trying to reach? What are their demographics (age, gender, income, education level, occupation, etc.)?

What are their interests, values, and beliefs? Are they customers, employees, stakeholders, or a combination of all three? Once you have a clear understanding of your audience, you can begin to tailor your message accordingly.

Gather data

There are many ways to gather data about your audience. One common method is to conduct surveys, either online or in person. Surveys can help you gather information about your audience's attitudes, preferences, and behaviors. You can also use social media analytics to track the conversations and interactions your audience is having online. Additionally, you can look at demographic data from sources such as the Census Bureau or industry reports.

Analyze the data

Once you have gathered data about your audience, you need to analyze it to identify patterns and insights. Look for common themes or trends that emerge from the data. Are there particular topics or issues that your audience cares about? Are there any challenges or pain points they are experiencing? What motivates them to take action?

Create audience personas

One useful way to synthesize your research is to create audience personas. These are fictional characters that represent your different audience segments. Each persona should include demographic information, as well as information about their needs, goals, and motivations. By creating personas, you can develop a deeper understanding of your audience and tailor your message to their specific needs.

Use your insights to tailor your message

Use the insights you have gained from your research to tailor your message to your audience. Consider what language, tone, and format will be most effective in communicating with them. Think about what kind of content will resonate with them and what kind of messaging will motivate them to take action.

Researching your audience is a critical step in developing a successful communication strategy. By identifying your audience, gathering data, analyzing it, creating audience personas, and tailoring your message accordingly, you can ensure that your message resonates with your audience and drives the outcomes you desire.

Chapter 4: Creating Your Brand Story

Defining Your Brand Identity

Defining your brand identity is a critical step in creating a successful and recognizable brand. It involves establishing the characteristics that set your brand apart from others and the values and beliefs that your brand represents. Here's a comprehensive and detailed explanation of what it means to define your brand identity:

Understand Your Target Audience: Before defining your brand identity, you need to understand your target audience. You should know who they are, what they like, and how they perceive your brand. This understanding will help you create a brand identity that resonates with your target audience and sets you apart from competitors.

Identify Your Unique Value Proposition: Your unique value proposition is what sets you apart from your competitors. It's the reason why your customers choose your brand over others. It's crucial to identify your unique value proposition so that you can incorporate it into your brand identity and messaging.

Develop a Brand Voice and Tone: Your brand voice and tone are the personality and character of your brand. It's how you communicate with your audience, and it's crucial to establish a consistent brand voice and tone across all channels.

Create a Brand Name and Logo: Your brand name and logo are the visual representation of your brand. Your brand name should be memorable, easy to spell, and unique. Your logo should be recognizable and represent your brand's values and characteristics.

Choose Your Brand Colors and Fonts: Your brand colors and fonts are an essential part of your brand identity. They should be consistent across all your branding materials, and they should represent your brand's personality and values.

Define Your Brand Messaging: Your brand messaging is the language you use to communicate with your audience. It should be consistent across all channels, and it should reflect your brand's values, beliefs, and unique value proposition.

Establish Your Brand Personality:
Your brand personality is the emotional and personal connection that your customers have with your brand. It's the tone of voice, the style of communication, and the overall perception of your brand. It's essential to establish a brand personality that aligns with your values and resonates with your target audience.

Create Brand Guidelines: Once you have defined your brand identity, you should create brand guidelines that outline all the visual and messaging components of your brand. These guidelines should be used to ensure consistency across all your branding materials.

Defining your brand identity involves a deep understanding of your target audience, your unique value proposition, your brand voice and tone, your brand name and logo, your brand colors and fonts, your brand messaging, your brand personality, and creating brand guidelines. By defining these elements, you can create a strong and recognizable brand that resonates with your target audience and sets you apart from your competitors.

Crafting Your Brand Story

Crafting your brand story is a crucial aspect of building your brand identity. Your brand story should reflect who you are, what you stand for, and what sets you apart from your competition. It is the foundation upon which all of your marketing efforts are built. A compelling brand story can help you connect with your target audience, build trust, and ultimately drive sales.

Here are some key steps to help you craft your brand story:

Define your brand identity: Start by defining your brand identity, including your values, mission, and vision. Think about what sets you apart from your competition, and what makes you unique.

Understand your audience: Next, you need to understand your audience. Who are they? What are their needs, wants, and pain points? How can your brand help them?

Develop your brand narrative: Once you have a clear understanding of your brand identity and your target audience, it's time to develop your brand narrative. Your brand narrative should tell a story that connects your brand to your audience. It should be authentic, engaging, and memorable.

Create a consistent brand voice: Your brand voice should be consistent across all of your marketing channels, including your website, social media, and advertising. This consistency helps to build trust with your audience and reinforce your brand identity.

Use visuals to enhance your story: Visuals can be a powerful tool in helping to tell your brand story. Use high-quality images and videos to help bring your brand narrative to life.

Continuously refine your story: Your brand story is not static, it will evolve over time. Continuously refine your story based on feedback from your audience, changes in the market, and new developments in your business.

Crafting your brand story is an ongoing process that requires a deep understanding of your brand identity and your target audience. By developing an authentic and engaging brand narrative, using consistent brand voice and visuals, and continuously refining your story, you can build a strong brand identity that resonates with your audience and drives success for your business.

Telling Your Brand Story Across Channels

In today's highly connected and information-driven world, a brand's success relies heavily on its ability to communicate its story effectively across different channels. Storytelling is a powerful tool that brands use to engage their customers and create a long-lasting emotional connection with them. However, telling your brand story effectively across multiple channels can be a daunting task, especially when the channels are diverse and the audience is fragmented.We will discuss the importance of storytelling in brand building and how to effectively tell your brand story across different channels.

Importance of Storytelling in Brand Building

Storytelling is not a new concept in brand building. Brands have been using stories to connect with their customers for centuries. However, with the rise of digital media and social networking, the importance of storytelling has increased significantly. A well-crafted story can help a brand differentiate itself from its competitors, create a connection with the customers, and build a loyal following. Here are some key benefits of storytelling in brand building:

Differentiation: A compelling story can differentiate a brand from its competitors. In a crowded marketplace, where multiple brands are selling similar products or services, a unique story can help a brand stand out and attract customers.

Emotional Connection: A well-told story can create an emotional connection with customers. Emotions play a crucial role in decision-making, and a story that triggers positive emotions can motivate customers to engage with the brand.

Memorable: Stories are more memorable than facts and figures. Customers are more likely to remember a brand's story than its product features or benefits.

Trust: Storytelling can build trust with customers. A brand that tells an authentic and relatable story can create trust and credibility with customers.

Effective Ways to Tell Your Brand Story Across Channels

To effectively tell your brand story across multiple channels, you need to develop a cohesive and consistent message that resonates with your target audience. Here are some key strategies to help you tell your brand story effectively:

Define Your Brand Story
The first step in telling your brand story is to define it. A brand story is not just about what you do, but it's also about why you do it. To define your brand story, ask yourself the following questions:

What motivated you to start your business? What is the purpose of your brand?

What values does your brand represent?

Who is your target audience, and what are their needs and desires?

By answering these questions, you can develop a clear understanding of your brand story and create a compelling message that resonates with your target audience.

Develop a Content Strategy

Once you have defined your brand story, the next step is to develop a content strategy that aligns with your brand's messaging and values. Your content strategy should include a mix of different types of content, including blog posts, social media posts, videos, and infographics.

When developing your content strategy, keep your target audience in mind. What channels do they use, and what type of content do they engage with the most? Understanding your audience's preferences will help you create content that resonates with them and helps you achieve your marketing goals.

Be Consistent

Consistency is key to effective storytelling. Your brand story should be consistent across all channels, from your website to social media to email marketing. Consistency helps build trust and credibility with customers and reinforces your brand messaging.

Use Visuals
Visuals can be a powerful tool in storytelling. Images and videos can help bring your brand story to life and make it more engaging for your audience. Use visuals to showcase your products, your team, and your brand values. Infographics can also be an effective way to convey complex information in a visually appealing way.

Engage with Your Audience
Engaging with your audience is an essential part of effective storytelling. Social media channels, in particular, provide a great opportunity to engage with your audience and build relationships. Respond to

comments, ask for feedback, and create polls to encourage engagement.

You can also leverage user-generated content (UGC) to enhance your brand story. UGC is content created by your customers, such as product reviews or social media posts featuring your brand. Sharing UGC on your channels can help build trust and credibility with your audience and showcase the real-life experiences of your customers.

Use Storytelling Techniques
There are several storytelling techniques you can use to make your brand story more compelling. Here are a few:

Use the hero's journey: The hero's journey is a storytelling framework that follows the journey of a protagonist as they overcome challenges and achieve their goal. You can use this framework to tell your brand story by showcasing how your brand helps customers overcome challenges and achieve their goals.

Create a narrative arc: A narrative arc is the structure of a story, which includes the exposition, rising action, climax, falling action, and resolution. Using a narrative arc can help create a sense of tension and keep your audience engaged.

Use metaphors: Metaphors can help simplify complex ideas and make them more relatable. For example, if your brand provides cybersecurity services, you could use a metaphor such as a "digital fortress" to convey the idea of protection and security.

Measure Your Results
it's essential to measure your results to determine the effectiveness of your brand story across channels. Use metrics such as engagement, reach, and conversion rates to evaluate the performance of your content and adjust your strategy accordingly.

Telling your brand story effectively across channels is essential for building a strong connection with your audience and differentiating your brand from competitors. To tell your brand story effectively, define your brand story, develop a content strategy, be consistent, use visuals, engage with your audience, use storytelling techniques, and measure your results. By following these strategies, you can create a compelling brand story that resonates with your audience and helps you achieve your marketing goals.

Chapter 5: Crafting Compelling Stories for Sales

Types of Stories for Sales

When it comes to sales, there are several types of stories that can be used to engage and persuade customers. Below are some of the most effective types of sales stories:

Success Stories: Success stories are stories that showcase how a product or service has helped a customer achieve their goals. These stories are particularly effective because they show real-world examples of how the product or service has helped others, which can be very persuasive to potential customers.

Personal Stories: Personal stories are stories that share personal experiences with a product or service. These stories can be particularly effective in building trust with customers because they show that the person selling the product or service has personal experience with it and can speak to its benefits from their own perspective.

Case Studies: Case studies are detailed accounts of how a product or service was used to solve a particular problem or achieve a particular goal. These stories are particularly effective in industries where customers are looking for concrete examples of how a product or service can help them.

Customer Testimonials: Customer testimonials are short statements from satisfied customers that describe their experience with a product or service. These stories can be particularly effective because they show that other people have had positive experiences with the product or service, which can be very persuasive to potential customers.

Brand Stories: Brand stories are stories that explain the history and values of a brand. These stories can be particularly effective in building brand loyalty and connecting with customers on an emotional level.

Vision Stories: Vision stories are stories that explain the vision and goals of a company. These stories can be particularly effective in industries where customers are looking for companies that share their values and are working towards a common goal.

Problem-Solution Stories:
Problem-solution stories are stories that explain how a product or service solves a particular problem. These stories can be particularly effective in industries where customers are looking for solutions to specific problems.

Overall, using stories in sales can be an effective way to engage and persuade customers. By using a variety of different types of stories, salespeople can appeal to different types of customers and build trust and loyalty with their audience.

Structuring Your Sales Story

As a salesperson, one of the most important skills you can possess is the ability to tell a compelling sales story. A well-crafted story can capture a prospect's attention, create an emotional connection, and ultimately lead to a successful sale. However, creating a sales story that resonates with your audience requires more than just throwing together a few talking points. It requires a thoughtful and intentional approach to structuring your story. We'll explore the key components of structuring a successful sales story.

Step 1: Define Your Objective

Before you start crafting your sales story, it's essential to define your objective. What do you hope to achieve with your story? Are you trying to generate interest in your product or service? Are you trying to overcome objections? Are you trying to close a sale? Once you've defined your objective, you can structure your story to achieve that goal.

Step 2: Identify Your Audience

The next step in structuring your sales story is to identify your audience. Who are you speaking to? What are their pain points? What motivates them? What are their goals? Understanding your audience is crucial to crafting a story that resonates with them.

Step 3: Develop Your Characters

The most effective sales stories include relatable characters that your audience can connect with. Think about the people involved in your story. Who is the hero? Who is the villain? Who are the supporting characters? What are their motivations? By developing your characters, you can create a narrative that your audience will find engaging.

Step 4: Define the Conflict

Every good story has a conflict, and your sales story is no exception. What is the problem that your product or service solves? What are the challenges that your customers face? Defining the conflict is crucial to creating a sense of urgency and demonstrating the value of your solution.

Step 5: Establish Your Value Proposition

Once you've defined the conflict, it's time to establish your value proposition. What is the unique benefit that your product or service provides? How does it solve the problem that your customers are facing? What sets your solution apart from the competition? Establishing your value proposition is key to convincing your audience that your solution is the right one for them.

Step 6: Craft Your Narrative

With the key components of your story defined, it's time to craft your narrative. Your story should have a clear beginning, middle, and end. Start by setting the scene and introducing your characters. Next, establish the conflict and demonstrate the challenges that your customers are facing. Then, introduce your solution and demonstrate how it solves the problem. Finally, close with a call to action that encourages your audience to take the next step.

Step 7: Use Visuals

Visual aids can be a powerful tool in enhancing your sales story. Consider using images, diagrams, or videos to demonstrate your solution in action. Visuals can help your audience better understand your solution and create a more compelling narrative.

Step 8: Practice, Practice, Practice

Once you've developed your sales story, it's essential to practice it. Rehearsing your story can help you refine your message and identify areas where you can improve. Consider practicing in front of a mirror, recording yourself, or practicing with a colleague. The more you practice, the more confident you'll feel delivering your story in front of a prospect.

Step 9: Personalize Your Story

Finally, it's important to personalize your story for each prospect. While the key components of your story may remain the same, you should tailor your narrative to address the specific pain points and goals of each individual prospect. Personalizing your story can help you build a stronger connection with your audience and increase the likelihood of a successful sale.

However, it's important to remember that storytelling is not a one-size-fits-all approach. Your sales story should be tailored to your specific audience, product, and objectives. While the steps outlined above provide a framework for structuring your story, you should always be willing to adapt and modify your approach based on the feedback you receive from prospects.

Additionally, it's important to remember that storytelling is not a substitute for building a strong relationship with your prospects. Your sales story should be one part of a larger strategy that focuses on building trust and establishing a connection with your audience. By combining a strong sales story with effective communication, active listening, and relationship building, you can increase your chances of closing more sales and building long-term partnerships with your customers.

Structuring your sales story is a critical component of successful selling. By defining your objective, identifying your audience, developing relatable characters, defining the conflict, establishing your value proposition, crafting a compelling narrative, using visual aids, practicing your delivery, and personalizing your story, you can create a story that captures your audience's attention and motivates them to take action. With a well-crafted sales story, you can differentiate yourself from the competition, demonstrate the value of your solution, and ultimately close more sales.

Using Emotional Triggers to Connect with Your Audience

Emotions play a crucial role in human communication, and incorporating emotional triggers into your content can help you connect with your audience on a deeper level. Emotional triggers are words, phrases, or images that elicit a specific emotional response from your audience. By using emotional triggers effectively, you can create a bond with your audience, build trust, and encourage them to take action.

Here are some tips for using emotional triggers to connect with your audience:

Identify your audience's emotional needs: Before you start creating content, it's essential to understand your audience's emotional needs. Ask yourself what emotions your target audience is likely to feel when they encounter your content. For example, if you're creating content for a parenting blog, you may want to focus on emotions such as love, frustration, and anxiety.

Use emotional language: Once you've identified your audience's emotional needs, incorporate emotional language into your content. For example, instead of saying, "Our product is great," say, "Our product will change your life." The latter is more likely to trigger an emotional response from your audience and make them feel excited about your product.

Tell stories: Stories are a powerful way to connect with your audience emotionally. Share stories that your audience can relate to and that evoke the emotions you want to trigger. For example, if you're a financial advisor, you could share a story about a client who was struggling to pay off their debt and how you helped them achieve financial freedom.

Use visual cues: Visual cues such as images and videos can be highly effective emotional triggers. Use images that evoke the emotions you want to trigger and make sure they're relevant to your content. For example, if you're writing a blog post about travel, use images of exotic locations that will make your audience feel excited and inspired.

Be authentic: Authenticity is key when using emotional triggers. Your audience will quickly spot if you're not genuine, and this can harm your credibility. Make sure your emotions are authentic and reflect your brand's values.

Use humor: Humor can be an effective emotional trigger, especially if it's relevant to your content and your audience's sense of humor. If you can make your audience laugh, you'll not only trigger positive emotions, but you'll also be more memorable.

Appeal to their values: People are more likely to feel emotional about things that matter to them. By appealing to your audience's values, you can tap into their emotions and build a stronger connection. For example, if you're a sustainability-focused brand, you can appeal to your audience's environmental values by highlighting the positive impact of your products on the planet.

Use social proof: Social proof is a psychological phenomenon that describes the tendency of people to follow the actions of others. By using social proof, you can trigger emotions such as trust and social validation. For example, you could share customer testimonials or user-generated content that highlights the positive experiences of your customers.

Create a sense of urgency: Urgency is a powerful emotional trigger that can motivate people to take action. By creating a sense of urgency in your content, you can trigger emotions such as fear of missing out

(FOMO) and a desire to act quickly. For example, you could use phrases such as "limited time offer" or "while supplies last" to create a sense of urgency.

Use sensory language: Sensory language refers to language that appeals to the senses, such as sight, sound, smell, taste, and touch. By using sensory language in your content, you can trigger emotions and create a more vivid and memorable experience for your audience. For example, if you're a food blogger, you could describe the taste and aroma of a dish in detail to evoke positive emotions.

Using emotional triggers is a powerful way to connect with your audience, build trust, and motivate them to take action. By understanding your audience's emotional needs, using emotional language, telling stories, using visual cues, appealing to their values, using social proof, creating a sense of urgency, and using sensory language, you can create content that resonates with your audience and builds a strong relationship.

Chapter 6: Building Trust with Storyselling

Building Rapport with Your Audience

Building rapport with your audience is essential in any communication setting. Whether you're giving a presentation, delivering a speech, or having a conversation, establishing a connection with your audience can help you build trust, credibility, and understanding. In this response, I will discuss comprehensively on building rapport with your audience.

Know your audience

Before you can build rapport with your audience, you need to know who they are. Research and gather information about your audience to understand their interests, needs, and values. This information can help you tailor your message to their specific needs, and show that you understand and care about their concerns.

Start with a positive tone

First impressions are important, and your opening statement sets the tone for the rest of your communication. Starting with a positive tone can help establish a connection with your audience and put them at ease. A positive tone can include humor, empathy, or excitement, depending on the situation and audience.

Be Authentic

People can usually detect when someone is being fake or insincere. So, it's essential to be yourself and let your personality shine through. Your audience will be more likely to trust and connect with you if you're authentic, honest, and transparent.

Use Body Language

Body language can help communicate your message and build rapport with your audience. Non-verbal cues such as smiling, making eye contact, and using gestures can convey your message more effectively and show your audience that you're engaged with them.

Ask Questions

Asking questions is an effective way to engage your audience and build rapport. It shows that you value their input and are interested in their perspective. Additionally, asking questions can help you understand your audience's needs and tailor your message accordingly.

Listen Actively

Active listening is crucial for building rapport with your audience. It involves paying attention to what your audience is saying, asking follow-up questions, and responding appropriately. By actively listening, you can show that you care about your audience and understand their concerns.

Share Personal Stories

Sharing personal stories or experiences can help you connect with your audience on a more personal level. It shows that you're human and have had similar experiences or struggles. Personal stories can also help illustrate your message and make it more relatable to your audience.

Use Humor

Humor can be an effective tool for building rapport with your audience. It can help lighten the mood, reduce tension, and make your message more memorable. However, it's essential to use humor appropriately and avoid offending or alienating your audience. Building rapport with your audience is a vital component of effective communication. By knowing your audience, starting with a positive tone, being authentic, using body language, asking questions, listening actively, sharing personal stories, and using humor appropriately, you can build trust, credibility, and understanding with your audience

Establishing Credibility

Establishing credibility is an essential element of effective communication. Credibility refers to the extent to which the audience perceives the speaker as trustworthy, knowledgeable, and competent. Without credibility, it can be challenging to persuade or influence an audience, and the message may not be received or accepted. Therefore, it is crucial to establish credibility to gain the audience's trust and ensure that the message is understood and accepted. We will discuss comprehensively on establishing credibility.

Knowledge and Expertise:
Demonstrating expertise in the subject matter is a critical factor in establishing credibility. It is essential to have a deep understanding of the topic, have relevant experience, and provide evidence to support claims. It is also important to keep up-to-date with the latest research and developments in the field.

Preparation and Organization: Being prepared and organized when delivering a message can enhance credibility. This includes having a clear and concise message, using credible sources, and being able to answer questions or challenges.

Confidence: Confidence in delivery can also enhance credibility. Confidence can be demonstrated through maintaining eye contact, speaking clearly and with authority, and projecting a sense of passion and enthusiasm for the topic.

Transparency: Being transparent and honest about limitations or areas where expertise may be lacking can also enhance credibility. This can help establish trust with the audience, and they are more likely to accept the message.

Empathy and Understanding: Empathy and understanding can help establish credibility, particularly in situations where the audience may be skeptical or resistant to the message. Demonstrating empathy and understanding can help establish a connection with the audience and help them feel that their concerns or objections have been heard and understood.

Consistency: Consistency in messaging, behavior, and actions can also enhance credibility. If the audience perceives inconsistencies in messaging or behavior, they may view the speaker as less trustworthy and less credible.

Reputation: Reputation can play a significant role in establishing credibility. A speaker with a reputation for being knowledgeable and trustworthy is more likely to be perceived as credible by the audience.

Nonverbal Communication: Nonverbal communication, such as body language and tone of voice, can also affect credibility. Nonverbal cues can convey confidence, sincerity, and authenticity, or they can undermine credibility if they are perceived as insincere or untrustworthy.

Ethos: Ethos is the persuasive appeal of the speaker's character or credibility. The audience is more likely to be persuaded by a speaker who is perceived as credible, trustworthy, and knowledgeable.

Audience Analysis: Understanding the audience and tailoring the message to their needs and interests can also enhance credibility. By demonstrating an understanding of the audience's concerns, interests, and perspectives, the speaker can establish credibility and build rapport with the audience.

Establishing credibility is critical to effective communication. By demonstrating expertise, being prepared and organized, projecting confidence, being transparent and honest, demonstrating empathy and understanding, maintaining consistency, having a good reputation, using effective nonverbal communication, appealing to ethos, and understanding the audience, a speaker can enhance credibility and effectively convey their message.

Using Stories to Address Objections

Using stories is a powerful way to address objections and persuade people to see things from a different perspective. Stories can be used to overcome objections by providing a relatable example or analogy that helps to illustrate your point and create an emotional connection with your audience.

Here are some ways in which you can use stories to address objections:

Use stories to illustrate your point: A
good story can help to illustrate a complex
point in a way that is easy to understand. By
telling a story that is relevant to the
objection you are addressing, you can help
your audience to see things from a different
perspective.

For example, if you are trying to sell a
product that is more expensive than the
competition, you could tell a story about a
customer who bought the cheaper product
but ended up spending more money in the
long run due to its lower quality and
durability.

Use stories to provide social proof:
People are more likely to believe something
if they see that others believe it too. By
telling a story about a satisfied customer or
someone who had success with your
product, you can provide social proof and
overcome objections related to skepticism or
doubt.

For example, you could tell a story about a customer who was skeptical about your product at first but was ultimately won over by its effectiveness.

Use stories to appeal to emotions: People make decisions based on emotions, not logic. By telling a story that evokes a strong emotional response, you can overcome objections related to fear, uncertainty, or doubt.

For example, if you are selling a security system, you could tell a story about a family who experienced a break-in and how the security system saved them from harm.

Use stories to create a common ground: Sometimes objections arise because the audience feels that the speaker is not relatable or does not understand their perspective. By telling a story that creates a common ground or shared experience, you can overcome objections related to differences in opinion or experience.

For example, if you are trying to sell a product to a specific demographic, you could tell a story about a customer who is similar to your audience in terms of age, gender, or background.

Use stories to address objections directly: Sometimes objections arise because the audience has a specific concern or question that needs to be addressed. By telling a story that directly addresses the objection, you can provide a concrete example and demonstrate that you have thought through the issue.
For example, if a customer is concerned about the safety of a product, you could tell a story about the rigorous testing and quality control measures that went into its development.

Using stories to address objections can be an effective strategy in various situations, such as in sales, marketing, or even personal communication. Stories can help to build rapport with your audience, create empathy, and make your message more memorable.

Here are some additional tips for using stories to address objections:

Make your stories relevant: When using stories to address objections, make sure the story you tell is relevant to the objection you are addressing. If the story is not directly related to the objection, it can lose its impact and effectiveness.

Keep it concise: When telling a story to address an objection, keep it concise and to the point. Long, rambling stories can lose your audience's attention and dilute the effectiveness of your message.

Use sensory details: Use sensory details to help your audience visualize the story and make it more memorable. By incorporating specific details like colors, sounds, or smells, you can create a more vivid and engaging story.

Use a strong opening: Start your story with a strong opening that grabs your audience's attention and draws them in. This can be a surprising fact, an emotional statement, or a dramatic scene that immediately captures their interest.

Use a strong conclusion: End your story with a strong conclusion that ties back to your message and reinforces the point you are trying to make. A strong conclusion can leave a lasting impression on your audience and help them remember your message.

In addition, it's important to remember that not all objections can be overcome with a story. Some objections may require a more detailed explanation or data to support your message. Be flexible and willing to adapt your approach based on your audience's needs and the situation.

Chapter 7: Storytelling in Different Sales Situations

Storytelling in Cold Outreach

Cold outreach is a sales and marketing technique that involves reaching out to potential customers or clients who have no prior relationship with your business. The goal is to introduce your brand and services to them, generate interest, and eventually convert them into paying customers.

One effective way to make cold outreach more engaging and memorable is by incorporating storytelling into your outreach efforts. Storytelling has been used as a tool for communication and persuasion for centuries, and it remains a powerful technique in modern marketing and sales.

Here are some ways storytelling can enhance your cold outreach efforts:

Makes your brand more relatable: Storytelling allows you to humanize your brand by sharing anecdotes and personal experiences that resonate with your target audience. By sharing stories that highlight your brand values and mission, you create a connection with your potential customers, making your brand more relatable and appealing to them.

Demonstrates your expertise: Storytelling also allows you to demonstrate your expertise and knowledge in your industry. By sharing stories of how you have helped other customers or solved similar problems, you showcase your skills and build trust with your potential clients.

Creates an emotional connection: Stories have the power to evoke emotions, and when used in cold outreach, they can create a more personal connection with your target audience. Emotionally engaging stories can help capture the attention of your prospects and make them more receptive to your message.

Enhances memorability: Storytelling also makes your outreach efforts more memorable. By using anecdotes and narratives to illustrate your message, you create a lasting impression that your potential customers are more likely to remember.

When using storytelling in cold outreach, it's important to keep the following tips in mind:

Understand your audience: Before crafting your story, it's essential to understand your target audience's needs, pain points, and interests. Use this information to create stories that resonate with them and address their specific challenges.

Keep it concise: While storytelling can be a powerful tool, it's important to keep your message concise and to the point. Avoid long-winded stories that may bore or confuse your prospects.

Use visuals: Visual aids such as images and videos can help enhance your storytelling and make it more engaging. Consider using visual elements in your outreach efforts to help illustrate your message.

Be authentic: Authenticity is key to effective storytelling. Avoid using fabricated stories or exaggerations that can damage your credibility and reputation.

Storytelling is a powerful tool that can enhance your cold outreach efforts by making your brand more relatable, demonstrating your expertise, creating an emotional connection, and enhancing memorability. When used effectively, storytelling can help you stand out in a crowded market and generate more leads and sales for your business.

Storytelling in Sales Presentations

Storytelling has become an essential part of sales presentations. It has become a way to engage and connect with the audience emotionally, which is crucial in creating a lasting impression and driving action. We will explore the importance of storytelling in sales presentations, the different types of stories, and how to incorporate them effectively.

Importance of Storytelling in Sales Presentations

Storytelling has the power to make a message more memorable, persuasive, and engaging. It can help bring dry data and facts to life and make them more relatable to the audience. A well-crafted story can help create an emotional connection with the audience, leading to higher engagement, retention, and action.

Moreover, storytelling can help differentiate a brand, product, or service from its competitors. It can help create a unique narrative and position the company in a way that resonates with the audience. Through storytelling, companies can establish trust, credibility, and a sense of community with their customers, leading to long-term loyalty and advocacy.

Types of Stories in Sales Presentations

In sales presentations, there are several types of stories that can be used to engage the audience and convey a message effectively. Some of the most common types of stories are:

Customer Success Stories: These stories showcase how the company's products or services have helped customers achieve their goals or solve their problems. They help build credibility and establish trust by demonstrating real-world applications and outcomes.

Personal Stories: These stories help build a personal connection between the presenter and the audience. They can be used to share personal experiences related to the product or service, building empathy and rapport.

Brand Stories: These stories showcase the company's mission, values, and history. They help create a unique narrative that differentiates the company from its competitors and creates a sense of community with the audience.

Analogies and Metaphors: These stories use comparisons to help the audience understand complex concepts or ideas. They help make the information more relatable and accessible to the audience.

Humorous Stories: These stories use humor to engage the audience and make the presentation more memorable. However, it's important to use humor appropriately and in a way that aligns with the company's brand and values.

Incorporating Stories Effectively

To incorporate stories effectively in sales presentations, there are several best practices to keep in mind:

Keep it relevant: The stories should be relevant to the product or service being presented and the audience's needs and interests. Avoid using stories that are tangential or irrelevant.

Use a clear structure: The stories should have a clear beginning, middle, and end. This helps the audience follow along and understand the message being conveyed.

Keep it concise: The stories should be concise and to the point. Avoid rambling or going off on tangents that can distract from the message.

Use visuals: Visual aids such as images, videos, or infographics can help reinforce the story and make it more memorable.

Practice, practice, practice: Practice telling the stories beforehand to ensure they flow smoothly and effectively. This can also help the presenter feel more confident and natural during the presentation.

Storytelling has become an essential part of sales presentations. It has the power to engage, connect, and persuade the audience, leading to higher engagement, retention, and action. By incorporating relevant and well-crafted stories, presenters can differentiate their company, establish credibility, and create a lasting impression with their audience.

Storytelling in Closing Deals

Storytelling is a powerful tool in business, especially in closing deals. Telling a compelling story that resonates with the potential client can be the difference between securing the deal or not. We'll discuss the importance of storytelling in closing deals, the elements of a good story, and how to create a narrative that resonates with your client.

Importance of Storytelling in Closing Deals

At its core, storytelling is about creating a connection with your audience. A good story can be used to communicate a message, inspire action, and build trust. When it comes to closing deals, storytelling can be used to create a sense of urgency, establish credibility, and highlight the benefits of working with your company.

One of the most significant advantages of storytelling in closing deals is that it helps to create an emotional connection with the potential client. When a client feels emotionally invested in your story, they're more likely to be receptive to your pitch and more likely to trust you. This trust is crucial in closing deals, as it can help to alleviate any doubts or concerns the client may have about working with your company.

Elements of a Good Story

To create a compelling story, it's essential to understand the elements that make up a good narrative. The following are the essential components of a good story:

Characters: Every good story has well-developed characters that the audience can identify with. In the context of closing deals, the client should be able to see themselves as the hero of the story.

Conflict: Conflict is an essential element of any story. In the context of closing deals, the conflict can be the challenges that the client is facing, and how your company can help to solve these challenges.

Resolution: Every story needs a resolution. In the context of closing deals, the resolution should be how your company can help to solve the client's challenges and achieve their goals.

Emotion: Emotion is a powerful tool in storytelling. By creating an emotional connection with the client, you can help to build trust and establish a relationship.

Creating a Narrative that Resonates with Your Client

To create a narrative that resonates with your client, it's important to understand their needs, challenges, and goals. The following are some tips for creating a narrative that resonates with your client:

Understand the Client's Needs: Before creating a narrative, it's essential to understand the client's needs. What challenges are they facing, and what goals are they trying to achieve? By understanding their needs, you can tailor your story to address these specific challenges and goals.

Use Storytelling to Highlight the Benefits: Use storytelling to highlight the benefits of working with your company. For example, if your company provides software that can help to streamline a client's workflow, use a story to illustrate how this software has helped other clients achieve similar goals.

Be Authentic: Authenticity is crucial in storytelling. Your story should be based on real-life experiences and examples that the client can relate to. Avoid using cliches or generic stories that don't resonate with the client.

Keep it Simple: The story should be simple and easy to follow. Avoid using jargon or technical terms that the client may not understand.

Storytelling is a powerful tool in closing deals. By creating a narrative that resonates with your client, you can build trust, establish credibility, and highlight the benefits of working with your company. To create a compelling story, it's essential to understand the elements that make up a good narrative, and tailor your story to address the client's specific needs, challenges, and goals.

Chapter 8: Measuring and Optimizing Your Storyselling Performance

Identifying Key Performance Metrics

Key Performance Metrics (KPIs) are measurable indicators that help businesses track their progress towards achieving their goals. These metrics are essential for businesses to identify and analyze their strengths and weaknesses, and make data-driven decisions to improve their performance. However, with so many metrics available, it can be challenging to identify the most critical ones for your business. Here are some steps to follow when identifying key performance metrics:

Define your business objectives:
Before identifying key performance metrics, you must first define your business objectives. What are the goals you want to achieve, and what are the most important factors that contribute to achieving those goals? For instance, if you want to increase sales, then revenue and customer acquisition rate might be essential KPIs.

Identify your target audience:
Who is your target audience, and what do they care about? Different metrics may be more relevant to different groups of people.

For example, if your target audience is investors, then financial metrics such as return on investment (ROI) might be more important than operational metrics.

Determine your data sources:
You need reliable data sources to track and analyze your performance metrics. Identify the sources of data you need to collect to track your metrics effectively. For instance, if you want to measure website traffic, you may need to set up Google Analytics or another website analytics tool.

Prioritize your metrics:
Once you have identified your business objectives, target audience, and data sources, you can start prioritizing your metrics. Focus on the most critical metrics that directly impact your business objectives. For example, if your business objective is to increase customer retention, then metrics such as customer churn rate,

customer lifetime value, and net promoter score (NPS) might be essential KPIs.

Establish benchmarks:

It's essential to establish benchmarks for your KPIs to track progress and set goals. Benchmarks are a way to compare your performance against industry standards, previous periods, or competitors. This helps you understand whether you're on track to achieving your goals or if you need to make adjustments.

Review and adjust your metrics:

KPIs are not static, and they may need to be reviewed and adjusted periodically. Review your KPIs regularly to ensure they are still relevant to your business objectives and target audience. If you find that a particular metric is not contributing to your business objectives, consider replacing it with a more relevant one.

Identifying key performance metrics is crucial for any business. By following these steps, you can identify the most critical KPIs that will help you track your progress towards achieving your business objectives. Remember to regularly review and adjust your metrics to ensure they remain relevant and effective.

Collecting Data and Analytics

Collecting data and analytics are two essential processes for any organization that wants to make data-driven decisions. Collecting data involves the process of gathering information, while analytics involves the process of interpreting that information to gain insights into various aspects of the organization. We will explore these two processes in more detail.

Collecting Data:

Collecting data involves gathering information from various sources. There are different methods of collecting data, including surveys, interviews, observations, and data mining. Data can be collected from various sources, such as customer interactions, social media, financial reports, and employee feedback.

One of the critical considerations in data collection is the quality of the data. The data collected must be accurate, relevant, and reliable. Data accuracy is essential because it ensures that the insights drawn from the data are correct. The relevance of the data ensures that it is related to the questions being answered. The reliability of the data ensures that it can be used to make accurate predictions.

Analytics:

Analytics involves analyzing the data collected to gain insights into various aspects of the organization. There are different types of analytics, including descriptive analytics, predictive analytics, and prescriptive analytics.

Descriptive analytics involves analyzing past data to gain insights into what happened in the past. This type of analytics is useful in identifying trends and patterns in the data. Predictive analytics involves analyzing past data to make predictions about future events. This type of analytics is useful in forecasting trends and predicting future outcomes. Prescriptive analytics involves using past data to make decisions about future actions. This type of analytics is useful in identifying the best course of action to achieve a particular goal.

The insights gained from analytics can be used to improve various aspects of the organization. For example, analytics can be used to improve customer satisfaction, reduce costs, increase revenue, and improve employee performance.

Collecting data and analytics are two essential processes for any organization that wants to make data-driven decisions. Collecting data involves gathering information, while analytics involves analyzing the data to gain insights into various aspects of the organization. These two processes are interconnected, and the insights gained from analytics are only as good as the data collected. Therefore, it is essential to ensure that the data collected is accurate, relevant, and reliable. With the right data and analytics, organizations can make informed decisions that lead to improved performance and increased profitability.

Continuous Improvement and Optimization

Continuous improvement (CI) and optimization are critical concepts in the field of business and management. The goal of CI is to continually evaluate and improve processes, products, and services, while optimization focuses on making those processes, products, and services as efficient and effective as possible.

Continuous Improvement:

Continuous improvement is the process of continuously identifying and implementing small improvements in a business process or system to achieve better results. It is a philosophy of making incremental changes that add up to substantial progress over time.

Continuous improvement involves the following steps:

Identify the problem: The first step in continuous improvement is to identify the problem or area for improvement. This could be a process that is inefficient, a product that is not meeting customer needs, or a service that is not providing value.

Analyze the problem: Once the problem has been identified, it is essential to analyze it in detail to understand the root cause of the issue. This may involve data analysis, process mapping, or other analytical tools.

Develop solutions: After understanding the problem, it is time to develop potential solutions. These solutions should be based on the root cause analysis and should be designed to eliminate the underlying problem.

Test the solutions: Once potential solutions have been developed, it is time to test them to see if they will work. This may involve pilot testing or simulation to see if the solution is effective.

Implement the solutions: Once the solution has been tested and refined, it is time to implement it across the organization. This may involve training, communication, and other change management activities.

Monitor and evaluate: Finally, it is essential to monitor the solution and evaluate its effectiveness. This may involve collecting data and metrics to ensure that the solution is working as intended.

Optimization:

Optimization is the process of making a process, product, or service as efficient and effective as possible. Optimization aims to improve the quality, speed, and cost-effectiveness of a process, product, or service.

Optimization involves the following steps:

Define the objective: The first step in optimization is to define the objective. This could be to reduce costs, improve quality, or increase efficiency.

Analyze the process: Once the objective has been defined, it is essential to analyze the process in detail to understand how it works and identify areas for improvement.

Develop potential solutions: Based on the analysis, potential solutions should be developed to optimize the process. These solutions should be designed to achieve the objective defined in step one.

Evaluate potential solutions: Once potential solutions have been developed, they should be evaluated to determine which solution is most effective in achieving the objective.

Implement the solution: Once the solution has been selected, it is time to implement it across the organization. This may involve training, communication, and other change management activities.

Monitor and evaluate: Finally, it is essential to monitor the solution and evaluate its effectiveness. This may involve collecting data and metrics to ensure that the solution is working as intended.

Continuous improvement and optimization are complementary concepts that can help businesses achieve their goals. Continuous improvement is a process of making incremental improvements over time, while optimization is focused on making processes, products, and services as efficient and effective as possible. By combining these two concepts, businesses can achieve continuous improvement while also optimizing their processes for maximum efficiency and effectiveness.

Conclusion

The Future of Storyselling

Storyselling is the art of using storytelling to sell products or services. It involves crafting narratives that capture the attention and imagination of customers and clients, helping them connect emotionally with a brand or product. Storyselling has become an increasingly popular marketing strategy in recent years, and its future is poised for continued growth and development.

One of the key drivers of the future of storyselling is the continued rise of digital media. With more people than ever before consuming content online, businesses have access to a vast audience that can be reached through targeted digital storytelling. This includes not just social media and digital advertising but also newer technologies such as augmented and virtual reality.

Augmented reality, in particular, has the potential to revolutionize storyselling. With AR, businesses can create immersive, interactive experiences that allow customers to engage with products and services in new and exciting ways. For example, a furniture store could use AR to allow customers to place virtual furniture in their homes before making a purchase, giving them a more realistic sense of what the product will look like in their space.

Another important factor in the future of storyselling is the growing importance of personalization. Customers are increasingly expecting personalized experiences from businesses, and storytelling is no exception. By using data analytics and artificial intelligence, businesses can create stories that are tailored to the individual interests and preferences of their customers, increasing the chances of engagement and conversion.

In addition to personalization, there is a growing interest in stories that promote social and environmental responsibility. As consumers become more aware of the impact their purchases have on the world around them, they are seeking out brands that align with their values. Storytelling can be a powerful way for businesses to communicate their commitment to social and environmental responsibility and connect with like-minded customers.

The future of storyselling will be shaped by advances in technology that we can't even imagine yet. With the continued development of artificial intelligence, virtual reality, and other emerging technologies, there is the potential for entirely new forms of storytelling to emerge. The key for businesses will be to stay on top of these developments and adapt their storyselling strategies accordingly.

The future of storyselling is bright and full of potential. As digital media continues to grow and new technologies emerge, businesses that can tell compelling, personalized, and socially responsible stories will have a distinct advantage in the marketplace.

Final Thoughts and Actionable Takeaways.

Storyselling is a powerful marketing strategy that involves using stories to engage customers, create emotional connections with them, and ultimately drive sales. The concept of storyselling is based on the idea that people remember stories better than they remember facts, and that stories have the power to evoke emotions and inspire action.

Final Thoughts on Storyselling:

People are emotional beings: One of the key principles of storyselling is the understanding that people are emotional beings. They make decisions based on emotions, not just facts and figures. By telling stories that resonate with your customers' emotions, you can create a strong connection that will make them more likely to take action.

Storytelling is an art: Storyselling is not just about telling any story. It's about telling the right story in the right way to the right audience. It takes creativity, skill, and practice to craft stories that engage and persuade customers.

Authenticity is key: Customers can sense when a story is not authentic, and it can backfire if they feel like they are being manipulated or lied to. The best stories are those that are true and genuine.

Measure your success: As with any marketing strategy, it's important to measure the success of your storyselling efforts. This can include tracking engagement, sales, and customer feedback.

Actionable Takeaways for Storyselling:

Know your audience: The first step in effective storyselling is to know your audience. This means understanding their needs, interests, and pain points. By knowing your audience, you can craft stories that will resonate with them.

Keep it simple: Stories that are too complicated or convoluted can be difficult to follow and may not resonate with your audience. Keep your stories simple and focused on a single message.

Use visuals: Visuals can help bring your stories to life and make them more memorable. Consider using images or videos to support your stories.

Be consistent: Consistency is key when it comes to storyselling. Make sure that your stories are consistent with your brand messaging and that they align with your overall marketing strategy.

Practice, practice, practice: Storyselling is a skill that takes practice. The more you practice, the better you will become at crafting and telling stories that engage and persuade your audience.

Storyselling can be a powerful tool for marketers looking to engage customers and drive sales. By understanding the principles of storyselling and implementing actionable takeaways, you can craft stories that resonate with your audience and inspire action.